BRIGHT IDEA BOOKS

KARLIE Kloss

by Samantha S. Bell

CAPSTONE PRESS
a capstone imprint

Bright Idea Books are published by Capstone Press
1710 Roe Crest Drive, North Mankato, Minnesota 56003
www.mycapstone.com

Library of Congress Cataloging-in-Publication Data
Library of Congress Cataloging-in-Publication Data is available on the Library of Congress website.
ISBN: 978-1-5435-5796-1 (library hardcover)
978-1-5435-6041-1 (paperback)
978-1-5435-5828-9 (eBook PDF)

Editorial Credits
Editor: Claire Vanden Branden
Designer: Becky Daum
Production Specialist: Colleen McLaren

Quote Source
p. 4, "Karlie Kloss on Wellness, Workouts, and Womanhood." *Vogue*, February 26, 2018

Photo Credits
AP Images: Joel Ryan/Invision, cover; Newscom: Demis Maryannakis/Splash News, 11; Rex Features: Giovanni Giannoni/Penske Media, 15, Kristina Bumphrey/StarPix, 22, Ray Tang, 8; Shutterstock Images: FashionStock.com, 6–7, 16–17, 31, littlenySTOCK, 24–25, magicinfoto, 5, Nata Sha, 18, 21, Ovidiu Hrubaru, 13, 27

Printed in the United States of America.
022019 001577

TABLE OF CONTENTS

CHAPTER 1

FROM CLOTHES to Coding

Karlie Kloss is a supermodel. She models clothes. She poses for photos. She also loves to learn. She believes education is a superpower. "I feel really strong when I'm challenging myself," Kloss said.

In 2014 Kloss took a class in **coding**. She wanted to learn more about technology. Most of the students in her class were men.

Karlie Kloss calls herself an inner science geek.

With the money she makes from modeling, Kloss donates to many different causes.

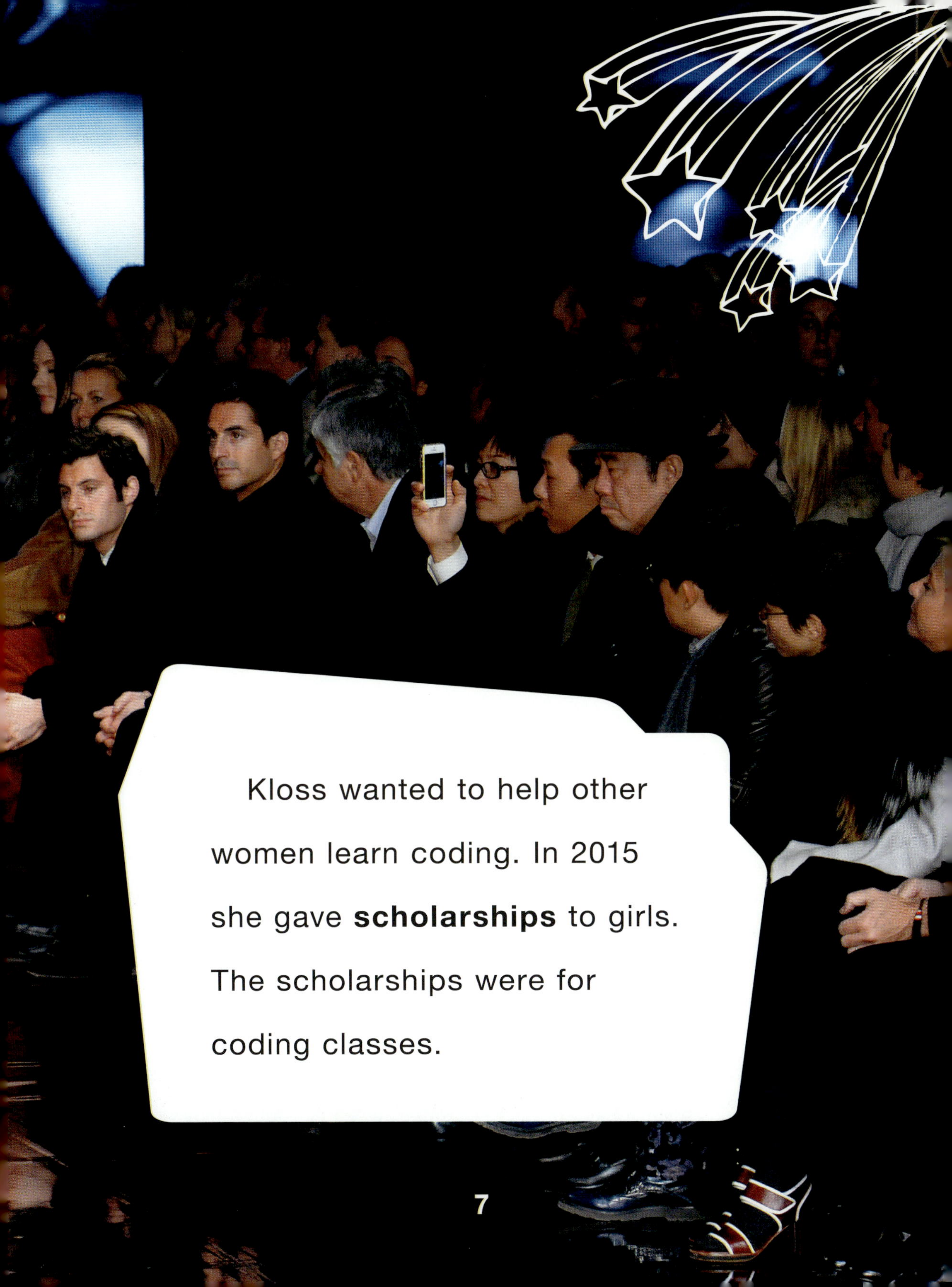

Kloss wanted to help other women learn coding. In 2015 she gave **scholarships** to girls. The scholarships were for coding classes.

Kloss has spoken to audiences about the importance of technology.

Then Kloss started a coding summer camp. Girls ages 13 to 18 could go. The camp was held in three cities. More camps are offered every year.

The camps are part of a **charity**. It is called Kode with Klossy. Kloss wants girls to become leaders in technology. She thinks they can change the world.

FUNDED BY KLOSS

The coding camp is free for the girls. Kloss pays for everything.

CHAPTER 2

CHANGING Goals

Kloss was born on August 3, 1992. Her family lived in Chicago, Illinois. Then they moved to Saint Louis, Missouri. Her father is a doctor. Her mother is an artist.

In school Kloss liked math and science. She wanted to be a scientist or teacher. She also thought about being a doctor. Kloss started ballet when she was 10. Her new love was dancing.

People told Kloss she was too tall to be a professional dancer.

A NEW DIRECTION

Kloss went to a model search when she was 13. She was already 5 feet 6 inches (168 cm) tall. Some fashion **scouts** saw her. They wanted her to model. She joined in their fashion show.

IMPORTANT SKILLS

Kloss' dancing background helps her model. Movement and rhythm are important skills. They are used in both dancing and modeling.

Most professional models need to be at least 5 feet 9 inches (175 cm) tall. Kloss reached that height in her teens.

CHAPTER 3

EARLY Success

Kloss started high school in 2007. She went to New York soon after school began. Her mother went with her. Then Kloss became a **runway** model. She was part of New York's fashion week. Kloss walked for a fashion company called Calvin Klein. She was just 15 years old.

Kloss was signed by Elite Model Management when she was 15 years old.

Kloss has worked for dozens of fashion designers.

Then Kloss' career took off. She began traveling around the world. Usually a family member went with her.

Kloss grew to be 6 feet 2 inches (188 cm) tall.

CAREER MODEL

Kloss had a busy first season. She walked in 64 fashion shows. She met many designers. Her photo appeared on a magazine cover.

Kloss graduated from high school in 2011. Then she moved to New York. She was ready to make modeling her career.

CHAPTER 4

MODELING and More

Kloss' success continued after high school. In 2011 she became a model for a popular clothing company. She began modeling for many designers. She has been a **cover girl** many times. She **represents** the beauty company L'Oreal.

Kloss has traveled all over the world to model.

Kloss often makes her cookies for fashion shows, photo shoots, and charity events.

Kloss is also a businesswoman. She worked with a bakery to make Karlie's Kookies. The cookies are dairy-free and **gluten-free**. Money from each sale helps feed hungry children.

Kloss also works with Frame Denim. This company makes jeans for tall women like Kloss.

Kloss still loves math and science. She decided to go back to school in 2015. She is a **part-time** student at New York University.

Kloss was in New York University's Gallatin School of Individualized Study program.

Kloss is more than a supermodel. She inspires young women around the world. She helps many girls become who they want to be.

Kloss inspires young women to learn and go after their passions.

GLOSSARY

charity
an institution or fund for helping someone in need

coding
a series of commands written for a computer to create a certain result

cover girl
a female model whose picture is on the cover of a magazine

gluten-free
something that does not contain gluten, a protein substance found in flour

part-time
only part of a usual school or work schedule

represent
to serve as a symbol of something

rhythm
coordinating movements with something you hear

runway
a narrow, flat platform used by models during a fashion show

scholarship
money given to a student to help pay for further education

scout
someone who searches for models

TIMELINE

1992: Karlie Kloss is born.

2005: Kloss enters a model search.

2007: Kloss gets her first job as a runway model at New York's fashion week.

2008: Kloss is on the cover of *Teen Vogue*.

2014: Kloss founds Kode with Klossy.

2015: Kloss becomes a student at NYU.

ACTIVITY

PUT ON A FASHION SHOW

Models can be male or female. They are all different ages. They wear the latest clothing styles in fashion shows. You can get friends and family together for your own fashion show.

Have the models decide what they will wear. They might choose something casual or sporty. They might choose something fancy or formal. They can put together a crazy, mismatched outfit too.

Decide where your runway will be. Those who are not modeling can be the audience. Have the models walk down the runway one at a time. You can even have a photographer with a cell phone or tablet take pictures.

FURTHER RESOURCES

Want to learn more about coding? Check out these books and websites:

Kode with Klossy
https://www.kodewithklossy.com

Wainewright, Max. *I'm a Scratch Coder.* New York: Crabtree Publishing Company, 2018.

Ziter, Rachel. *Coding Games from Scratch: 4D An Augmented Reading Experience.* North Mankato, Minn.: Capstone Press, 2019.

Want to try designing fashions like supermodels wear? Take a look at these sources:

Bolte, Mari. *Fab Fashions You Can Make and Share.* North Mankato, Minn.: Capstone Press, 2015.

Kids Think Design: Fashion Design
http://www.kidsthinkdesign.org/fashion/index.html

INDEX